we lived like KINGS

G.M. MANZI

Raw Earth Ink

2022

This book is a work of poetry.

Copyright 2022 by G.M. Manzi

All rights reserved. No part of this book may be reproduced or used in any manner without express written permission from the author except in the case of quotations used in a book review in which a clear link to the source of the quote and its author is required.

First paperback edition June 2022

ISBN 979-8-98504-067-8 (paperback)

Published by Raw Earth Ink
PO Box 39332
Ninilchik, AK 99639
www.taracaribou.com

*For Ma, Dad, my sister Beck,
and my loving pitbull Tatty.*

"I have never listened to anyone who criticized my taste in space travel, sideshows, or gorillas. When this occurs, I pack up my dinosaurs and leave the room."
                                                            -Ray Bradbury

"Writers may be disreputable, incorrigible, early to decay, or late to bloom, but they dare to go it alone."
                                                            -John Updike

"At the risk of appearing foolish, a writer sometimes needs to be able to just stand and gape at this or that thing---a sunset or an old shoe---in absolute and simple amazement."
                                                            -Raymond Carver

"There's no one thing that's true. It's all true."
                                                            -Ernest Hemingway

Preface

You hold in your hands a printed copy of my debut book, which is itself an accomplishment I thought would never, ever see the light of day. Why a poetry collection, one may ask? Why not a novel, or short story collection, or memoir? To which I answer---why not? I don't consider myself a poet, and I definitely don't consider myself an artist to any degree as I find that label a tad bit pretentious. I try to consider myself a storyteller but sometimes I feel this too is inaccurate. If anything, I consider myself to be both a muser and an observer. I write what I see, feel, and occasionally believe whether it be sober, drunk, or stoned. I then put my own little spin on it and, if it doesn't bore or disappoint me? I figure it may just entertain you, the reader, and if you *are* entertained, or moved to tears, laughter, anger, introspection, or befuddlement---then I've done my job as a writer. All I need to do is write, and present, I don't need to explain anything. It was Chekhov, after all, who is credited as saying "The role of the artist is to ask questions, not to answer them."

I like that. I like the idea of readers wondering what the hell I'm babbling about and me being the only one that knows the truth. It tickled Joyce to frustrate his readers too. I know the who's, the what's, and the when's of what the inspiration was and I like knowing I can choose whether or not to ever reveal what's fact based and what's bullshit based. You're adults with, I'm assuming, grown up minds of your own. I'll present you with the words, the story, the musing, the observation---but Chekhov was right, I'm not here to hold your hand. I've done the dirty work---the rest is up to you.

I'll let you in on this secret only---my musings come from everywhere and anything. It could be random thoughts throughout the day about dinner or work, a memory of an event, person, or conversation twenty years ago I thought forgotten, how a cocktail may taste, a woman's outfit on a first date, the harshness of the wind, ratty old boxers, a dog's vomit, and if I know you personally, then likely you as well. Raymond Carver may have been best at that. Carver said in an essay of his titled, simply enough, *On Writing*, that it's best to find "commonplace things" and use "commonplace but precise" language (ALA Hemingway) to gift things like "...a fork, a stone, a woman's earring---with immense, even startling power."

I like that too. I love writing about the everyday as seen through my mind's eye. Whenever people hear the phrase "the simple things" they no doubt imagine a plain living people like the Shakers, Quakers, Amish, or Mennonites and in turn believe "simple" to be code for "boring." But, as Bilbo Baggins tells us, "...it is no bad thing to celebrate a simple life." Maybe it's a regional thing, as I grew up in a small rural town in upstate New York (and as a New Yorker I want to be clear, "upstate" NY is not Westchester. It begins at the base of Greene County and runs north until you hit Canada), and I went to a small school, and I went to a small Sunday school, and I remember creeks and fallen leaf piles and snow covered everything and popsicles in Summer and dandelions covering every green surface in Spring. Or perhaps it's because I can sit on my porch and remember my college roommates a certain way after a sip of rum-and-coke, or ponder Jungian synchronicity immediately after looking at a stranger's footprints in the snow, or feel a connection to the Netherworld or to God when I watch the swirls and dances of cigar smoke. That comes easier to me than writing about witches and warlocks, dragons or demons.

I could go on and on about influences and inspiration but this is supposed to be a brief introduction that maybe gives you a bit of insight into what I'm about, and what you're about to read. This little tome almost never happened. It exists through a recipe of work hard and practice even when I thought it was pointless to continue this hobby of mine, a bit more luck than I'd care to admit, and, I'd like to think, by being myself and not caving to trends.

I've made mention of and referenced Chekhov and Carver, and although I've tried to follow their example and incorporate enough of them into myself without shamelessly pilfering, it's John Updike I've always felt most kinship with. He may be (along with Andre Dubus) the quintessential Northeast small town writer. The Rockwell of Letters. His three page story *"In Football Season"* changed the way I read, the way I write, and the way in which I view and observe life. He said in an introduction to *"Early Stories"* that his ultimate aim was to "...give the mundane it's beautiful due." I love that. I relate to that. Bill Watterson said through *Calvin and Hobbes* (another massive influence on me in the vein of Updike that deserves its own essay) that "There's treasure everywhere," and I want my readers to get as close as they can to seeing how snow days, people, love, a cloudy day, or puddles of rain water open the floodgates to what it is I see and feel.

I am no John Updike or Bill Watterson (no one can be either of them) and I do not have the inherent gifts of the masters. Hell, there's a lot I don't have. I have no friends in artist or literary circles, no independent wealth, no movie star good looks, and no trophies, awards, or certificates of appreciation to hang on my wall. I'll have this book on my shelf though. Even if it's my last, it's still my first. I have no intention to stand on the shoulders of giants and piggyback on what they've already done, and I have no expectations or pipe dreams that end with me standing shoulder to shoulder as equal with the giants. But I can at least walk with the giants, now, that right there is a feather in my cap, even if they *are* baby steps. Not bad for a small town kid from Nowhere, New York who's a grocery store butcher by trade, is it?

                              -G.M. Manzi

To Savor the Barley

I've never shared a drink with Dad.
Not a whiskey, not a beer---
Hell I caught a dirty look when
I had champagne at my sister's wedding.
Isn't it a rite of passage?
For the son to savor the barley
with the father?
But he refuses.
He calls my drinking a problem.
The truth is---he doesn't want
to see I am no longer eight years old.

But I'm still me, Pa.

I didn't think it'd be too much to
have bought you a two hundred dollar
bottle of bourbon when you retired
so we could've sat on the porch on a
cool Summer night and clinked our glasses.
Sipping slow to enjoy the magic that fifteen years
in a charred oak barrel produces in a spirit.
We wouldn't need to talk.
There wouldn't be a need.
The moment would speak for itself.
It'd make up for those talks that
should have been but never were.
I'll bring the drink, you bring the ice.
It's not too late, we have all the time
in the world still.

The Fount

I'd one day love to
spin a tale from yarn
weaved from that which
brings me joy, peace,
and serenity.

But that well has seemingly run dry,
and the fount of creativity
is always, and unfortunately, better fed
by the spring from which flows my miseries,
my misfortunes,
and my unforgiving hatreds.

My Hemingway

I have an idea, she told me once,
move in with me? Maybe?
You can quit your shitty job,
I make enough to support us,
don't worry about that.
You can focus on your writing and be my Hemingway.
And every weekend we'll get stoned and
drunk or trip and we'll have amazing sex
whenever we can and want to.
Just think about it?

I told her of course I would.
I'd have to be stupid not to.

I was that stupid,
and I didn't think about it at all.

As Dylan Croons

I kick my slippered feet up
on the porch railing.
The sky is clear and the air is
pleasantly, and surprisingly,
crisp for early July.

The candle I lit for the lantern glows.
Bundled up in a light throw blanket,
I sit on my Adirondack chair,
sipping from a bottle of Guinness as
Dylan croons through my speakers
how he's sick of love.

    (You destroyed me with a smile
    while I was sleepin')

I ask myself if I need her---
if I truly, honestly, need her.
I will miss her, sure, but no.
No I do not need her.

Going on Thirteen

Had they not realized the condom broke,
he thought the other day,
that kid would have been twelve going on
thirteen right about now.

They did realize it though,
and she asked for a twenty so that
she could run to CVS for the morning after pill.
Crisis averted.
Their young lives could continue.

The kid who wasn't born,
he thought, was the lucky one.

Taste of Smirnoff

It's pushing midnight and
I know who to expect soon.
I get up and prepare a strong vodka-
cranberry for when she walks through the door and
throws her leather jacket over my chair.

Oh, for me, Love? she'll say, upon seeing the drink.
And look, she adds, I didn't even have to ask.
She winks at me before taking a deep sip,
which she follows with an even deeper kiss in which
the taste of Smirnoff, mixed with cranberry,
remains on her lips and is now on mine.

There haven't been any midnight visits
for a while now---
but the taste of her vodka soaked
tongue still lingers.

Her Ankle Bracelet

I could feel her ankle bracelet rubbing
against the back of my calf.
That's the detail that sticks out
to me when I think about her.
Maybe that's because she insisted on
always keeping the lights off.

I can't tell you how she looked when she moaned,
or how her Double Ds may have bounced up and down,
or if her long brown hair fell over her
shoulders the way I imagined it did.

But what I can tell you is this---
how she sounded,
how she smelled,
how her hands rubbed my chest
as she'd wrap her legs around mine and
pull me inside her.

And damn it,
wouldn't you know---
I can tell you what that
ankle bracelet felt like on
the back of my calf.

The Wheat Field

I'm chasing her through a wheat field,
that's the dream I had the other night.
Even though I never saw her,
I knew exactly who it was I was chasing.
She was in a Jeep,
and I was on foot but somehow I
still managed to keep up.
It felt as if she wanted to get away but,
at the same time, she didn't want to lose me---
she wanted me to catch her.

The most vivid thing I recall, though,
is the field itself---
how vast it was, how endless.
How it shimmered like gold.
Impossibly gold.
The most impossibly golden wheat field
that ever did grow.

I kept up the chase until,
suddenly, I realized she wasn't driving---
and then it hit me who in fact was,
and I gave it up.

As the Jeep drove off and out of site,
a strong wind blew,
and I stood standing alone amongst
the golden wheat.

Breakfast

Woke up to the sound of rain on
a chilly mid-September morning.
We're in the final throes of what was
a tough Summer, giving way to
the first glimpses of Autumn.

My clock reads nine in the morning.
I make a pot of coffee and an egg
sandwich on a hard roll with ham and cheese.
I take the coffee black,
and sip it while it's still piping hot.
It warms my bones and
it warms my soul.

I sit on the couch with my coffee
and breakfast and I close my eyes.
Briefly, the world around me stops existing,
save for the sound of rain hitting the
grass and the fallen orange leaves.

I try and forget last night.
I try to forget the dark place
I found myself in.
I try to forget about sincerely
wishing I was dead.
Then I remember I don't want to be dead,
not really.
I don't wish to feel that way
again for a very long time.

Certainly not now,
and certainly not during breakfast.

To the Girl Who Thought I Was Sleeping

As she buries her face in my chest
and cries quiet tears,
thinking I'm asleep,
I'm actually wide awake,
but saying nothing.
I let her cry.

Although I may act distant or
appear indifferent,
I'd like her to try and
remember this anyway---

I know what it is that
makes you cry tonight,
and the thing you don't believe
is the thing I know and the thing I promise...

You'll be fine dear.
You'll be just fine.

Haiku to a Night Out

Very drunk, I sit
outside on a bar's front steps.
Please, don't touch. Might hurl.

One of Them

It's been just another day.
Another crap day at work.
Another bill I forgot to pay.
Another fight where the ex
called me an asshole.
Another prospective job turning me down.
Another day bereft of hope.
Another day wondering
why, oh why, do I bother?
Just another day in a string of them.

> *Do you know how many people
> died today*, the voice says to me,
> *and you weren't one of them?*

I answer yes,
and go to bed knowing there's
a chance tomorrow may not be
just another day.

Conundrum

Too tired to continue,
too stubborn to die.
A conundrum, Oh Life!
Still will I try.

Two Day Trip

The year is 1990.
Dad and I are driving from New York
to Tennessee to help move my Aunt back.
I have recently turned four years old.
I bring a few action figures---
a Hulk Hogan, a Batman, and Spider-Man,
probably a G.I. Joe or two.
I don't say anything the entirety
of the two day trip.
I just sit there and play with my men.

The year is 2020.
Dad still laughs about how
I don't say anything the entirety
of the two day trip.
In a little world of your own, he says laughing,
should have stayed four forever.

Don't I know it Dad, don't I know it.

Nothing

I got nothing today.
No motivation.
No ambition.
No desire.
No drive.
Nothing.
No inclination to do anything
at all that in any way would be
considered the least bit productive---

Except to stay home in bed and
continue to look at the silver moon
through my window.

In the Same Position

I woke to find her still in my arms,
in the same position we fell asleep in.
It was a dark morning,
and raining very heavily.
Closing my eyes and listening
to the downpour, my mind begins to wander---
to the past due credit card and cell phone bills.
To the money I don't have and
shouldn't have spent the night before.
To the promotion they said was all but
mine but didn't get.

I realize at that moment, though,
none of that meant a damn.

The difference today is
that she was there next to me---
still in the same position we fell asleep in.

Holding the Door for an Elderly Veteran

Walking into the bank today I
noticed an elderly gentleman with
a cane walking ever so gingerly
towards the door.
Being a good, young Samaritan,
looking out for and respecting our elders,
I got the door for him.
I saw he was wearing a Vietnam
Veterans cap (it may have said Airborne),
bless this man's soul if that is true.
He thanked me,
and I went to open the
second door to the lobby for him.

I God damn got it,
is what he said to me.

I flipped the old bastard off
behind his back and wished
him to drop dead.

Just Like Jim

He'd had too much gin the other night
and was depressed as shit.
He takes his phone out to get ahold of her.

>I miss you.
>I miss us.
>I thought you'd save me.
>Thought you'd save me...
>>*a love that I thought would save me.*

Just like that, he thinks of Jim
Croce telling the operator to
forget about this call,
and so too does he.

>Tonight, and hopefully from
>here on out,
>just like Jim,
>there's no one there I really
>want to talk to either.

Their House on Depot Lane

He wished he could be the little
kid he saw earlier that day
playing in the snow with his mother.
He was walking the dog and he paused
a spell to quietly observe them.

The kid was four, maybe five, or six.
The mother? Maybe late twenties,
or early thirties.
It was just the two of them in their
little enclosed back yard at
their house on Depot Lane.
Lost, were they, in the carefree world of
a fresh, bright snowfall.
He was certain their only worry was
if the cocoa would still be hot
when they got back inside.

He remembered that's how he
and his own mother once were,
and would never be again.
He stood there unnoticed,
with the dog beside him getting antsy,
for about ten minutes before he
felt moisture in his eyes,
and he quickly walked away.

Mom, What the Fuck Was I Thinking Going Through With This?

Sometimes, Honey,
she said,
the best decision you
can make for yourself
is masked as both the hardest and
most terrifying one to make.

Watch Some Basketball

I was going to have to drop
a cool five hundred to replace the alternator,
literally two weeks after dropping
a cool six to replace the fuel injector.
My mood was sour,
and all I wanted to do was sit
on the couch and feel sorry for myself.
Seeing the stress continuing to build
on my face, Dad chimes in---

> Just relax and watch some basketball,
> he tells me, it's the playoffs---gotta
> root for that Tim Duncan baby.
> Have that girl of yours over.
> Eat some pizza.
> Don't worry about crap you can't change.

He pats me on the shoulder, walked away,
and that was that.
Nothing Earth shattering.
Nothing you'd frame and hang
over your desk in the office.
Anybody could have told me that,
literally anybody.

Only it didn't come from anybody.

In the Company of Gods

With unlit pipe in hand,
on a clear and brisk night,
I try to relax on the porch and
clear my head but, as usual,
my thoughts meander to places
I really wish they wouldn't.

I gaze up into the starry night sky,
and I see that tonight both Venus and Jupiter have
seen fit to grace us with their presence.
With this I am reminded that we are always
in the company of Gods.

I strike a match and light the
cherry vanilla leaves packed into the bowl,
and the smoke rises to greet them.

Muse

I'm afraid one day you'll
write about me, she said to him,
with concern in her voice and
worry in her eyes.

Of course I'm going to,
he told her,
but don't be nervous about it---
you've been a most wonderful muse.
It was the most honest thing he ever told her.

Fifteen Minutes

He didn't notice the cap wasn't
screwed on when he went to
shake the OJ.
Juice went everywhere.
He knew it sure as hell wasn't
himself who didn't screw the cap on.
He got a ration of shit from his
mother for the mess that was made.
When he protested, he got another
ration of shit for pointing the
finger at someone else.
He had only been awake
for fifteen minutes.

Bagels at Work

They got us bagels at work the other day.
I ate four, free of guilt, in one sitting---
two everything, one plain,
one sesame seed.
I dipped them in cream cheese
as one dips chips into salsa.

How can you do that
to yourself? I was asked by a
coworker whose name I didn't even know.

Easy, I said,
none of us lives forever.

A Picture of You and Me

I have a picture of you and me that,
for some reason,
I've kept all these years.
This was before your first,
and second, and third kid.
This was when I was a college freshman,
and the future from the view of my
young mind's eye was still as sweet
and ripe and bountiful as the
vineyards of Napa Valley.

It was a future I naively believed you
would be in forever and ever.
Before the sole evidence
that you existed at all was
the picture of you and I that,
for some reason,
I've kept all these years.

Disagreeing with Robert Frost

According to acclaimed New England
bard Robert Frost---
the woods are lovely, dark, and deep.
God damn liar.

What he fails to mention are
how sinister, woeful, and ruinous they are.
They have mocked me with every
step and turn and bend---
and I wish to travel them no longer.

Here, here and now,
shall I lay me down to sleep.

Gets Me Off

The only thing
now that gets
me off is making
others feel like shit and
hate me as much as I
feel like shit
and hate me.

Always You

It's a crisp and crystal
clear night and I got
my feet kicked up on
the porch, piano jazz playing
through my speaker,
a freshly cracked bottle of
Guinness in my hand, and you,
always you,
right there on my mind.

Musings From the Day I Turned Two and Thirty

There will be no more water balloon fights.
No more superhero sheet
cakes from the local grocery store.
No more pizza and sleepovers with friends talking
about our crushes until two in the morning before
Dad yells from his bedroom to go to sleep.
No more Ma making Special Birthday Breakfast
(Whatever you'd like, Honey).
No more cupcakes before recess.
No more friends and relatives gathered
'round to sing and gift you money and action figures.
No more Grandma around to call and
in her throaty voice exclaim
"Happy Birthday Sweetheart!!!"

Forever sad that time's now passed.
Forever grateful it was there to exist at all.

What Does it Say About Me, Then

That a whiskey and gin soaked,
stale cigar smelling dive
out of an O'Neil play with
Tom Waits as its piano man
is what I describe to people
as my happy place?

Cherry

I sit myself up in bed with a
giant bowl of ice cream.
Three generous scoops of black raspberry,
layered with a bountiful serving of
ReddiWhip, nuts, and marshmallow topping.
I, ever so slowly, spoon massive amounts
into my maw and let it melt before gulping
it down in delight as I try not to think of
the ultrasound picture she sent me earlier.
I'm not sure why she thought to show me.
I should have said I couldn't care less but,
as my tears earlier proved,
that would have been a lie.

While stuffing my face,
I ponder Life's bizarre twists and turns---
remembering how she was supposed to be
my one and only.
Destiny. That was the word she used.
Her and I were destiny, she'd say before
kissing me sweetly.

> *No matter what, you and I are destiny.*

All it took to change destiny was another man
cumming inside of her.
Being shown what was growing
in her belly was the cherry for the
sundae I had just eaten.

I bring the bowl to the kitchen sink
and rinse it out while shedding another
quick tear or two.
Awe well, I think, as I dry my eyes and bowl
before I throw caution to the wind and go
to the freezer for more.

Your Tell

All I want, truthfully,
is for you to smile.
That's the long and short of it.
If I can make you smile,
you never have to tell me
you love me, never have to
admit to me your hidden desires,
or anything that may leave
you feeling vulnerable.
Your smile, dear, has always been your tell---
and it's worth more than any
words from you could ever be.

The Cardinal

I'm shoveling the driveway
in the cold of the Great Northeast because,
wouldn't you know it,
that goddamn snow blower shit the bed.
I got my big Carhartt coat and flannel pants on and
I'm cursing under my breath because no one,
save for Dad, ever gleefully
enjoyed shoveling the snow from a hundred foot
driveway in the bitter cold.

I'm trying my damnedest
to get the job done when,
looking out into the back yard,
I saw one lone cardinal land on a branch,
maybe fifty feet away from me.
The fire engine red of his form appearing so suddenly
on the stark white landscape nearly blinded me.

I couldn't help but pause to admire him.
I don't know why it affected me like it did,
or why I stopped so long to look at him.

Then it hit me.

There I was---
huffin' and puffin'
and pissin' and moanin'
and whinin' and cryin' about my busted
snow blower, and the job,
and the shitty love life,
and the bills,
and not having had any coffee yet.

All the while, there that cardinal sat,
alone on his perch.
Looking around with his chest puffed out
as if to say
World, do your worst, I do not give a damn.

And then, just like him,
I didn't give a damn either.

We Lived Like Kings

I'm sitting on the porch with my feet
up on the railing, having a smoke,
when the gentlest of Summer breezes caresses my face and
spirits me away to a life a decade or so ago that
I'm ashamed to have forgotten I once had.
A life where I lived on the west coast of Florida,
Saint Petersburg to be precise,
and I shared my apartment with my girl Teri.

I swear, it never seemed like I had more than
thirty bucks to my name until the next
two week pay period came.
She had even less.
But, y'know, it never felt like a struggle.
I made rent every month,
we had enough to stay fed and living,
and somehow we'd have enough left over
for decent liquor, smokes,
and the occasional night out for dinner.

But most of our time was spent on my balcony
on clear, cool nights I'm convinced don't
exist anywhere else in the world except in West Florida.
We'd have a drink in one hand, usually cheap wine or cheap
rum and cokes, and a joint in the other that we'd
pass between us while laughing about nothing.
When we'd had enough, we'd go inside and
make love with the sliding balcony door open
so we could feel the soft ocean breeze,
and maybe a hint of rain, coming in from the Gulf.

We were both a hair over twenty-one.
I had thirty bucks to my name.
Thirty damn dollars.
We lived like kings, her and I.
We never thought we'd ever be wealthier.

The Snow Day, a story told in verse

As expected, the blizzard is here in force.
Twelve to twenty expected and only
to get heavier as the day goes.
I snow blow, and bring in wood for the stove.
Then I let the dog out to romp around
and piss before the snow gets too heavy.
She gets a little too excited and knocks
me down before trotting away.

Rather than get up,
I lie on my back and let the snow land and
melt on my face.
It's nearing midday,
and it's beginning to fall steadily

After a few rather relaxing minutes of lying motionless,
looking up into the vast and infinite white sky,
my entire body jolts as if struck by
a thunderbolt.
Something has happened in me.
I've made a decision,
a bold decision.
I go inside and call my boss---

Darren, I say, I'm taking
a snow day.

I pause to collect myself,
my voice is shaking I'm so giddy...

> *I'm going to call up my friends*
> *and it's gonna be just like it was*
> *when we were kids.*
> *I'm gonna tell them to bring their saucer sleds and*
> *snowsuits,*
> *their scarves and their hats,*

> their gloves and their boots.
> And we're gonna play and laugh and
> snowball fight until we're called home to supper.

I continue, excitement building as I speak...

> After that, I'll rest a bit and thaw by the stove
> with some crackers and peanut butter
> before I put my snowsuit back on.
> But wait---what's this?
> Mom's coming outside with me!
> She's planning to chase and tickle me like
> she used to until I run out of breath and, gasping,
> beg for it to end.

Now I bet you think it ends there, I tell
my boss, but no. No it doesn't...

> See what happens next, Darren, to my amazement,
> is that Dad and my sister will come home.
> They both put on their snowsuits and
> Dad even dug out his goofy red felt cowboy hat for the occasion.
> I haven't seen that thing on his head in ages.
> He'll somehow muster the strength of old to
> pull my sister and me down and up the hill of
> our dead end road on the
> shitty blue plastic sled he dug out of the shed.
> The snow will be heavy by then and
> we'll jump around and wrestle in the
> two feet of cold white cushion until
> we're red in the face and exhausted.
> Then we'll go inside for hot cocoa that
> Ma's prepared before I lay down for a deep,
> heavy sleep with a smile I haven't
> had on my face since my age was in the single digits.

Today, I tell my boss,
is a special sort of snow day.
The past has come roaring with the North wind

to take my hand and guide me back
to a time gone by that, somehow, still exists.
I'd be stupid not to take advantage of this.

Of course, he tells me,
take the day and enjoy it.
Hell, he continues, himself sounding excited,
I was thinking of doing that very thing myself!

While my visions were real,
that conversation with my boss never happened.
My parents are twenty years divorced,
longer than they were married.
Mom has bad knees and has trouble walking long distances.
Those friends I had are no longer rambunctious children.
I am no longer eight years old and am, in fact,
closer to being forty than I am to being a teenager, even.

What happens is I lie to my boss about not seeing a plow all day,
even though one cleared our road about a half hour ago.

He understandingly, but begrudgingly,
lets me stay home,
and although I don't get to have a child's
snow day, the adult one consisting of hot black coffee,
naps, looking out the window,
and plenty of reading is an alternative I don't object to.

Later in the day, as the light outside begins to darken,
I see something faintly, through the increasingly heavy snow,
out in the back yard.
I put on my heavy Carhartt overalls and bomber hat,
spike my coffee, and turn on the outside lights before
venturing out to sit on the porch stairs that face
the back yard and the woods.

That's when, on my mother's life, I saw them.

By the forest's edge about sixty yards from
where I sat, through an ethereal barrier
made from the falling snow, they stood in formation like
stoic, ghostly Spartans---

My childhood friends, snowsuits on and
saucer sleds at the ready like Roman Legionnaires.
At the center, leading them,
was my mother with her still-good knees,
my sister when she was four, in her pink and yellow jacket,
and my dad, with his goofy red felt cowboy hat.
Standing between them in the center of the phalanx,
is eight year old me.

My friends in unison turn their heads to
look back, alert, as if hearing something.
They face me and wave quickly before turning and
running into the woods, as if called home to supper.

My dad and sister wave next,
it's exuberant and silly, just like they've always been,
They both turn and they take each other's hand,
then playfully rush off, shitty plastic blue sled in tow.

My mother's wave is slower---
melancholic and bittersweet.
She kneels to say something to my younger
self and kisses him on the head.
She slowly gets up, favoring her right knee,
then waves once more to me before
turning, and gingerly makes her way to the woods.

My younger self turned to go with her,
before pausing briefly and turning back to me.
Through a quivering lip and tears I didn't even
realize were rolling down my cheeks,

I hear my pleas over the
chilling blizzard wind.

>Please don't go.
>Please don't.
>Not you.
>For the love of God not you too.

My younger self raises both hands in the air
and waves them over his head,
as if to say
>Look at me! I'm right here!
>I'm just over here!

He stops, and gives a parting wave.
I return it with a wave of my own.
He does a final about face towards the woods,
and he vanishes with all the others.

I remain seated for I don't know how long,
my gaze remaining fixed on the tree line.
The coffee has long gone cold,
three more inches has accumulated,
and at some point I snap out
of it and brush the snow off of me.
I don't mind the cold, though,
and I stay put a little while longer.

I'm grateful I took the day for myself,
regardless of the tears it ended in.
It was a lovely, dreamy day.
For a sweet spell, I was eight years old again,
and I felt the purest form of love and
happiness I ever knew in the fresh, white landscapes and
hills of my small rural town at the edge of the world.

When I get up to leave, I raise my hand once more towards
the tree line and slowly wave,

and through the falling snow and silence,
that beautiful, beautiful Winter silence,
I say out loud, to those gentle specters out there, listening,
the only thing that there is to say---
                Until we meet again.

What He Knew Would Happen

He figured they'd be in bed
together somewhere around midnight---
and he knew exactly what
would be happening.

She was, after all, drinking
with her fella whom she hadn't
seen in twelve days.
Of course, because he was dumb and
jealous and a caveman and just had to know,
he asked---and what he knew would
happen did indeed happen

All she said was "yes,"
but, as he was once the fella,
and not so long before this,
he knew what she did to him,
and precisely how she did it.
He knew all her tricks to please.

You lucky bastard, he thought,
as he started rubbing one out to
the thought of them together,
You lucky God damn bastard.

The Wise Man and the Sad Man

If you were to change one thing,
the wise man told the sad man,
you would change everything.

What if, replied the sad man,
that's why you want to change
that one thing?

The wise man said nothing,
but looked with sympathy at the sad man,
and the sad man looked down
to hide his face.

The wise man knew there was only
one thing he could do---
he hugged the sad man,
and the sad man hugged him back.

What the Silence Tried to Tell Me

I stand outside my house as
the snow falls steady throughout the neighborhood.
Silver crystals reflected in the streetlight cover the road.
I think of you and all that should have been,
and all that now will never be.
Then, of course, I think of life and where I am in it.
Of the loneliness, the crippling loneliness,
these last few months have brought and
how you'd comfort me were you still around.

> *It's okay,* I hear faintly echoed
> amongst the Winter's silence,
> through her delicate, chilling winds...
> *It's okay*

I don't know what will be okay, and
I'm doubting whether I heard anything at all.
That it's my mind playing tricks,
until the glistening white that now blankets what
was the day before a brown, cold, and dead landscape
finds a path to my racing, anxiety riddled heart and
slows the beating to a crawl.
I understand what the silence tried to tell me,
I understand what will be okay.
I bow my head to Winter before I turn to
walk back inside the comforts of my home.

Sand

I was told,
not as long ago as it feels,
in a love letter I still keep in my
desk beneath a worn notebook, some pens,
and a half empty pack of gum...

> *Forgetting you is like holding*
> *onto sand and not losing any---it's impossible.*

And, like the sand in the wind or
taken by the waves, she too has vanished.

The Crack of a Bat

Too many poets, writers, artists, and other
creative types believe all their inspiration and
works must come from the depths of the heart and soul.
Sadness, heartbreak, overcoming obstacles, debauchery,
finding oneself, this, that, and the other...

Though I am as guilty as the next guy or gal
of finding inspiration in life's garbage heap,
it doesn't always need to be like that,
and that's not where this poem comes from.
Not today.

Today this poem comes from looking outside
my window on a late Spring day.
I'll write about how there's *just* the right amount
of cloud cover to let out *just* the right amount of Sun.
That there's just the perfect amount of breeze to
carry the freshness of the season and all of life so
that when you close your eyes you'd think
you were at Fenway Park or Camden Yards---
and you can swear on your mother you could hear
the crack of a bat somewhere off in the distance.

Yes, I am tired, and frustrated, and exhausted,
and full of my life's own hatreds---
not today though.
Today? I'm happy to say the heart is contented.

Presents, or
A Christmas Poem in Prose

I am thirty-four years old.
My sister is thirty,
but every Christmas is the same---

Though my parents are twenty years divorced,
Dad usually stays the night and wakes us at seven
in the morning to *Must Be Santa* by Mitch Miller
and The Gang before putting the cinnamon buns in the oven.
Ma puts the coffee on, my Uncle shows up around 7:30
after getting his own coffee from the gas station,
I take my seat on the couch, and my sister takes
her spot on the floor to dig through and
hand out everybody's presents.

Around this time Dad usually quips something along
the lines of Why the hell are there so many presents, or
How old are you two?
The two of us don't really ask for anything anymore,
it just sort of happens.
Yes I understand how silly it must seem to you all,
the image of two fully grown thirty year olds
excited by Christmas morning with their
sixty year old parents.

I ask you this---is that not the magic of Christmas?
I'm convinced those that do not still have a shred
of belief left in it are dead inside.
More presents for me, then.

Seasons

It is you.
You, who are my falling golden leaves
on a brisk and chilly Autumn day.

You, who are my soothing voice
that echoes across the landscape on the Winter wind.

You, who are my steady rain that melts away
in Spring the snow that's lingered.

You, who even on the hottest days
cools me with a mid-Summer sunset.

You, who are my seasons.
You, who are my beginning,
my middle, my end, and my rebirth.

Vision of a Winter Wind

She was in my vision of a Winter wind.
Light snow blew across her face and melted
in her dark and wavy hair.
She wears a long black coat of infinite midnight.
She stands in a meadow of tall, dry grass besides
a winding brook fed by tears of ice.

She turned to me and her gaze,
dark eyes that know all the answers,
met mine and her lips curved into a melancholic
smile that said nothing but told me everything.

I'm sorry, I heard myself say, as I dropped
to my knees and begged to be forgiven.
My cries came from deep within,
behind an iron door to which she held the key.
The wind blew in forceful gusts as I wrapped
my arms around her legs and
cried away a sadness I had forgotten I had carried.

The wind grew fierce, it pierced my heart and
she would not shield me from it as she once did.
When I looked up to meet her gaze again,
her eyes told me all I needed to know.

The wind howled in sorrow,
ice and tears remained flowing in the brook,
I remained crying on my knees,
and her melancholic smile stayed.

Pictures

All of those pictures of us,
hanging on the walls,
one day will be just that.

Find Me in the Ethers

Find me in the Ethers.
I promise, when you find my
hand you will know it.
Then you and I will dance the
dance that flows with time,
and we will be forever bathed in
the spectral colors of all those
who came and danced before.

Of Stupid Grins and Stevie Ray Vaughan

She and I lie next to each other
on the bed, very stoned, with stupid
grins on our faces and our eyes fighting
to remain opened.

The calming scent of pot smoke lingers in the air.
Who's this? She asks of the song that
currently plays through my speakers.
It's "Lenny", I say, by Stevie Ray Vaughan.
She lets out a heavy sigh that you
can sense released any and all stress.
It's nice, she says softly, almost in a whisper,
as she gently grabs my hand.

Yeah it is, I reply, and softly squeeze
her hand back. Yes it sure is.

Cheshire Cat Grin, or
To Dad on His Sixtieth

There's a picture I found of Dad and I from
when I was a boy.
I was three, maybe four years old.
He must have been around my age then that I am now.
He's got me up on his shoulders as he walks.
This was during a time before my sister existed,
back when he would call me Bitabuddy,
which stood for "Little bit of a buddy."

He's got on his gorgeous pea coat he got in the Navy,
and is wearing the Cheshire Cat grin of his that
I have come to inherit.
I wonder what he was smiling about during
that walk in the Fall of 1989.
I believe it was elation.
He had, after all, just finished his military service.
Armed with the knowledge he had
escaped a motherless and impoverished childhood fed on a
steady diet of daily scoldings, beatings, and boiled beef and
gravy.
Or being left with relatives, friends of the family, and
acquaintances, all who
must have wondered what the Hell
was going on while my Grampa went
out to gallivant and sow his wild oats.

If I could reach him through that picture,
would I tell him that in thirty years' time that
you will violently hurt your back and
get booted from the police force, divorce your wife,
never reconnect with your insane father or absent mother,
and eventually sport hair resembling Ben Franklin? Yes.
And I'd tell him he did well.

I'd get to tell him he retired early after busting
his ass for the local electric company for
twenty-five years,
and that life thereafter would be naught but
road trips,
tee times, and early bird specials at the diner
with his retired golf buddies.
I'd get to tell him that by the time he hits
the milestone of sixty, he'd have weathered
the storm completely.

I wonder how much wider that Cheshire Cat grin
would get if he knew that during that walk
in 1989.
My guess? As wide as it still is today.

Acknowledgments

Apart from my family, whom this debut book is dedicated, there are a few people I need to thank and acknowledge and give a shout out to for one reason or another, whether they read this or not. I will also probably forget a few people; I apologize, please do not feel slighted.

First and foremost is Jessica Leigh McCarthy, she knows why I'm thanking her, and that stays with us. My Uncle Mike for inspiring me to think beyond convention. My Auntie Slim, Uncle Jim, and my cousins for great Christmas dinners and for always being positive constants in my life. My Radio and Television Broadcasting instructors from my days at Herkimer County Community College, Bob Gassman and Douglas Flanagan, for showing me that a different path taken does not mean a bad path taken. My high school football and track coach at Chatham High, Jim Spock, who both saw something in me and helped to mold me despite my not being All-Star material. My Italian 101 professor at SUNY Albany, Patricia Keyes, who failed at teaching me another language but pushed me to my sometimes painfully uncomfortable limits and made a better person out of me because of it. My publisher, Tara, at Raw Earth Ink for taking a chance on me and turning dream into reality.

Finally, a time saving but nevertheless sincere and genuine thank you to all friends and friendly acquaintances that have enjoyed my pieces before publication and who encouraged me not to give up the hobby. Without the support from a core group of people, no one would be holding this weighty tome in their hands.

www.ingramcontent.com/pod-product-compliance
Lightning Source LLC
Chambersburg PA
CBHW051715040426
42446CB00008B/897